# THE ANCIENT EGYPTIANS

## Jackie Gaff

*p*

# CONTENTS

This is a Parragon Book
First published in 2002

Parragon
Queen Street House
4 Queen Street
Bath BA1 1HE, UK

Copyright © Parragon 2002

*Produced by*

David West ♟ Children's Books
7 Princeton Court
55 Felsham Road
Putney
London SW15 1AZ

British Library Cataloguing-in-Publication Data

A catalogue record for this book is available from
the British Library.

ISBN 0-75257-819-7

Printed in Dubai

*Designers*
Julie Joubinaux, Rob Shone

*Illustrators*
Kevin Maddison, Pete Roberts (Allied Artists)

*Cartoonist*
Peter Wilks (SGA)

*Editor*
James Pickering

# ANCIENT SPLENDOUR

**F**OR 2,500 YEARS, ancient Egypt was one of the world's richest and most powerful nations. Its time of greatness began nearly 5,000 years ago, and ended about 2,500 years ago. In their lands along the banks of the River Nile, the ancient Egyptians built vast temples for their gods and splendid palaces for their rulers. But their most famous monuments were the pyramids.

**CAN YOU BELIEVE IT?**
*Nothing lived in the desert.*

**NO.** There were lions and other wild animals in the desert. It was a dangerous place, and few ancient Egyptians went there.

**Towering tombs**
*The pyramids were built as vast tombs to protect the dead bodies of ancient Egyptian rulers, and important nobles and officials. They were so well constructed that some are still standing today.*

**YOU MUST BE JOKING!**
The ancient Egyptians called their country *Kemet*, meaning the Black Land, after the rich black river mud in which farmers grew their crops. The desert was called *Deshret*, meaning the Red Land.

## THE LAND OF THE NILE

Egypt is a hot country, where it hardly ever rains. The people of ancient times settled beside the River Nile because it supplied the water they needed to live and grow food. Apart from the narrow strips of green farmland beside the Nile, Egypt is mainly dry sandy desert.

Giza
Memphis
EL FAIYUM
RED SEA
River Nile
Valley of the kings
Karnak
Thebes

Flooded area

# FABULOUS PHARAOHS

**T**HE ANCIENT EGYPTIANS called their king the pharaoh, and they believed he was the living son of a god. He was head of the priesthood, the government, the lawcourts and the army – the most powerful person in the entire country, in fact. The pharaoh didn't run everything by himself, though. There were lots of officials to help him.

**YOU MUST BE JOKING!**
Pharaohs were allowed to have more than one wife at a time, and some of them had lots of children. Egypt's mightiest pharaoh, Ramesses the Great, had 96 sons and 60 daughters!

**Royal rig-out**
*The pharaoh's ceremonial clothes included a red-and-white crown and a false beard. The tail of a bull or a giraffe was fixed to the back of his belt, and he carried crook and flail sceptres.*

## TUTANKHAMUN'S TREASURE

Tutankhamun didn't live long enough to make his mark as pharaoh – he died when he was only 17. He's become famous since the 1920s, when his tomb was discovered packed with glittering treasures, including a solid gold face mask.

### CAN YOU BELIEVE IT?
*All the pharaohs were men.*

**NO.** A few were women. The most successful was Hatshepsut, who even wore the pharaoh's false beard.

# GLORIOUS GODS

**T**HE PEOPLE of ancient Egypt had hundreds of gods and goddesses. Some were more important than others, though, and the chief god was Amun-Re. His temple at Karnak was the biggest and wealthiest in ancient Egypt.

**CAN YOU BELIEVE IT?**
*Priests bathed the god's statue daily.*

YES. They washed it and then dressed it in clean clothes at dawn.

## ANIMAL SPIRITS

Many of the Egyptian gods were shown with an animal's head or body. Bastet, for example, was the goddess of cats, dancers and musicians. The cow-headed Hathor was the goddess of love, while the crocodile-headed Sobek was the god of water.

The Egyptians believed their temples were the homes of the gods, and ordinary people weren't normally allowed inside them to worship.

**YOU MUST BE JOKING!**
Priests had to wash several times a day to purify themselves for visiting the god's statue. They also had to shave their heads and eyebrows.

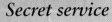

*Secret service*
*At the temple's heart was a shrine, with a statue of the god inside. Only the pharaoh and his priests were allowed here. Priests visited the statue every day, to bring fresh food and drink for the god.*

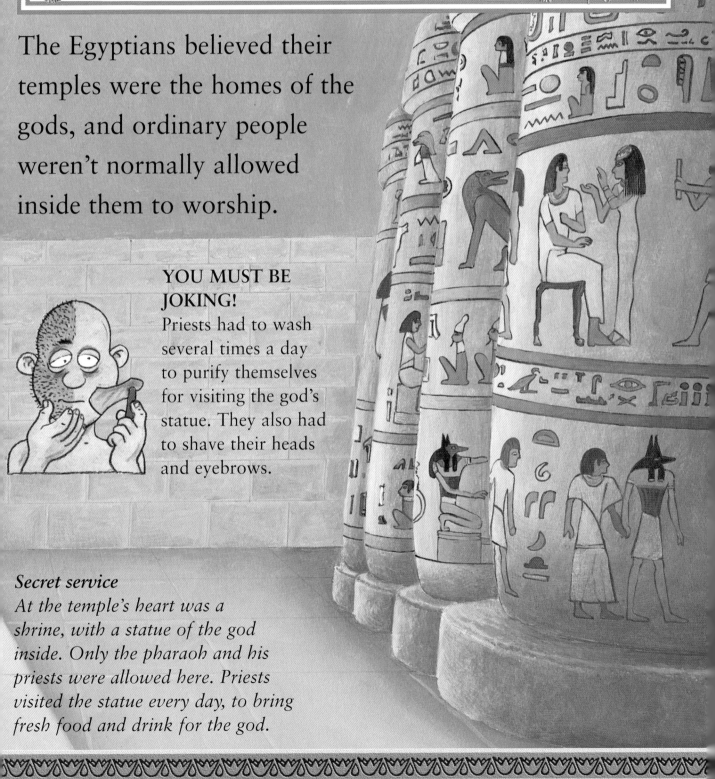

# MAKING MUMMIES

**T**HE EGYPTIANS BELIEVED that the dead travelled to another world, the Afterlife, where they still needed their bodies. Mummification was a process that dried a dead body out, stopping it from rotting away and saving it for the Afterlife. The Egyptians were so skilled that their mummies have lasted for thousands of years – they can still be seen today in museums all around the world.

*Dead ending*
*The Egyptians used a kind of salt called natron to dry dead bodies out. This stage lasted 40 days. Then the body was rubbed with special oils and wrapped in fine linen bandages. Finally, the mummy was placed in a coffin and buried.*

### YOU MUST BE JOKING!
The Egyptians believed that if the dead were buried properly, they would be able to eat, drink and move around in the Afterlife. So they buried them with everything from food and drink to clothes and games.

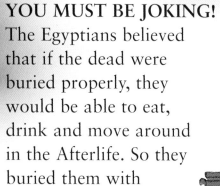

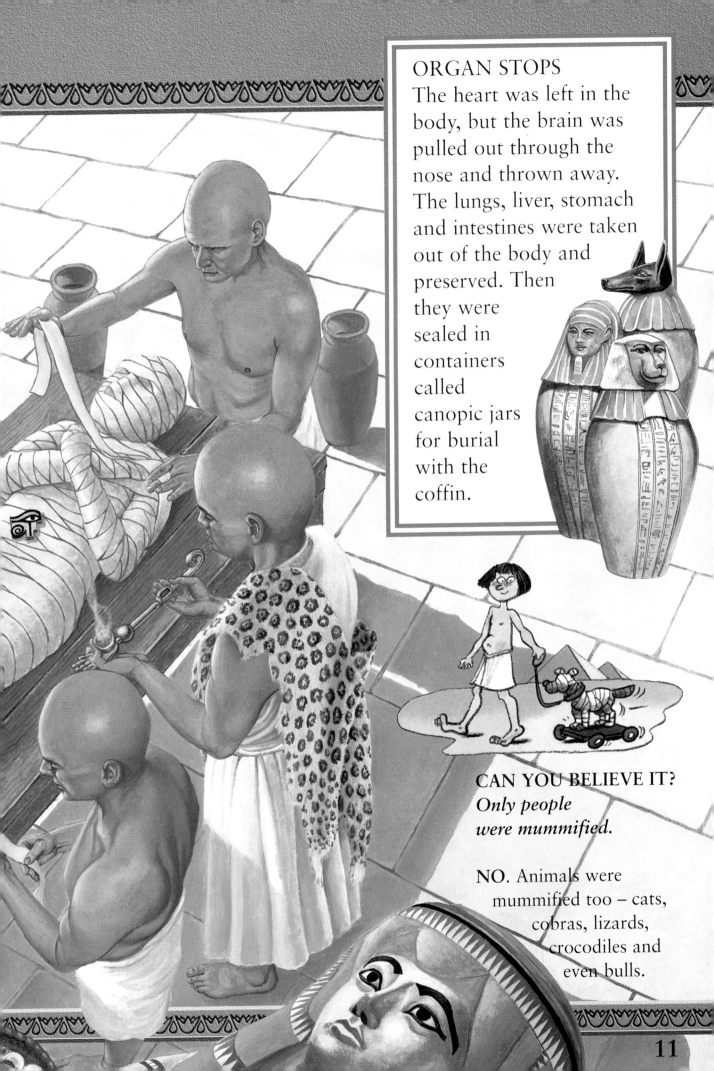

## ORGAN STOPS

The heart was left in the body, but the brain was pulled out through the nose and thrown away. The lungs, liver, stomach and intestines were taken out of the body and preserved. Then they were sealed in containers called canopic jars for burial with the coffin.

**CAN YOU BELIEVE IT?**
*Only people were mummified.*

**NO.** Animals were mummified too – cats, cobras, lizards, crocodiles and even bulls.

# PYRAMID POWER

**T**HE BIGGEST ANCIENT Egyptian structure is the Great Pyramid at Giza, built for Pharaoh Khufu about 4,500 years ago. It towered 146.5 metres above the desert sands – as high as a 40-storey tower block! It was covered in creamy white limestone, which was polished until it sparkled in the hot desert sunlight.

*Hard labour*
*It took more than 100,000 workers over 20 years to build the Great Pyramid. Beneath its casing, it was constructed from huge granite blocks, some weighing as much as 50 tonnes (or 10 elephants).*

**CAN YOU BELIEVE IT?**
*Pharaohs were always buried in pyramids.*

**NO.** So many pyramids were robbed that later pharaohs were hidden inside underground apartments, tunnelled into rocky hillsides.

## YOU MUST BE JOKING!

It took some time for the Egyptians to perfect the pyramid shape. The first one was stepped, while another experiment had bent sides. One early pyramid even fell down just after it was finished.

## TOMB RAIDERS

All sorts of hidden entrances and false passages were designed to try to stop robbers breaking into the pyramids and stealing the precious goods buried with the pharaoh. Nothing worked, though. More than 80 pyramids were built, and they were all robbed.

# FARMING THE LAND

IF PHARAOHS WERE AT THE TOP END of Egyptian society, farmers were at the bottom. They worked away growing the crops that everyone needed for food.

Farming in Egypt was made possible by the Nile. Every summer, the river rose and broke its banks, flooding the fields with life-giving water and rich dark river mud. When the floodwaters went down, the farmers began to sow their crops.

**CAN YOU BELIEVE IT?**
*Farmers had to pay taxes.*

**YES.** They had to hand over a share of their crops every year as a tax payment to the pharaoh.

## YOU MUST BE JOKING!

Farmers even had to work during the flood season. Not on the land, though – they had to slave away on one of the pyramids or another of the pharaoh's latest building projects.

### Water management

*Canals and ditches ran around farmers' fields to channel water to their growing crops after the floods went down. A lifting device called a* shaduf *was used to raise river water into the canals.*

### BUMPER HARVEST

The main crops were wheat and barley, used to make bread and beer. Flax was important too, because it was woven into linen for clothes. Farmers also kept animals and grew fruit and vegetables, including dates, figs, grapes and melons, and beans, leeks, lettuce and onions.

**O**RDINARY EGYPTIANS LIVED on bread and vegetables, with beer to wash their meals down. Sometimes they ate fish, but meat was mainly for the wealthy.

*Fun and games*
*Guests at a feast wore cones of perfumed fat on their heads, which slowly melted to keep them cool and smelling sweet. They were entertained by musicians, singers and dancers.*

RECIPE FOR SUCCESS
The ancient Egyptians didn't have fancy kitchens or cooking equipment. Food was stored in baskets or clay pots. Grain was ground into flour between stones, and bread was baked in a clay oven. Meat was roasted over an open fire or grilled on a brazier.

Nobles and other wealthy people ate all sorts of exotic meals, and they really knew how to throw a party. A feast menu might include meat dishes made from antelope or herons.

**YOU MUST BE JOKING!**
Egyptian beer was so lumpy that people sucked it up through a wooden strainer. Studies of mummies have shown that bread was so gritty that it wore people's teeth away.

**CAN YOU BELIEVE IT?**
*Guests sometimes ate so much at a feast they were sick.*

**YES.** A servant would bring a sick bowl, then the guest would carrying on partying!

# DRESSED TO KILL

**W**EALTHY EGYPTIANS could spend hours getting ready for a feast. After a wash and a massage with scented oils, it was time to put on their make-up. Men and women painted their eyes and wore lipstick. Then came a wig made of real human hair and clothes made of the finest pleated linen. Last, but not least, were masses of beautiful jewellery.

*Staying in style*
*Fashions changed, but by 3,500 years ago wealthy Egyptian men were wearing a kilt under a shirt-like top for special occasions. Women wore a long tunic-like dress, often with a cloak on top.*

**CAN YOU BELIEVE IT?**
*Egyptians were vain about their looks.*

**YES.** They even mixed up potions to cure baldness, dandruff and spots.

## GLITTERING PRIZES

The ancient Egyptians loved jewellery, and both men and women decorated themselves with rings and earrings, as well as necklaces, bracelets and anklets. Even pet cats wore rings in their ears and noses!

## YOU MUST BE JOKING!

Egypt is such a hot country that children often wore no clothes at all. Young boys' and girls' heads were shaved, except for a single plait on one side.

**M**OST EGYPTIANS WORE rough linen clothes and lived in simple houses. An ordinary family's home would have two to three rooms on the ground floor, with an outside staircase leading to a roof terrace.

*Keeping cool*
*A shady roof terrace was an ideal place to relax after work. In summer, it was the coolest place to sleep. Houses had thick walls to keep the heat out in summer and the warmth in during winter.*

**CAN YOU BELIEVE IT?**
*Egyptian houses had bathrooms.*

**YES.** There were no taps or running water, but wealthy families had a bathroom with a washing slab and a sand toilet.

Although very few trees grew in Egypt, there was plenty of mud. So houses were built from mud-bricks baked hard in the hot sunshine.

**YOU MUST BE JOKING!**
Egyptians didn't have cupboards. Things were stored in boxes and chests, instead. There were tables and chairs, but no sofas. The rich had beds but no soft pillows – they laid their heads on a wooden head-rest!

LIVING THE HIGH LIFE
The homes of the wealthy were larger, with many more rooms. These were decorated with beautiful wall paintings. Outside there was a garden, often with a fish pool, and outbuildings for servants and animals.

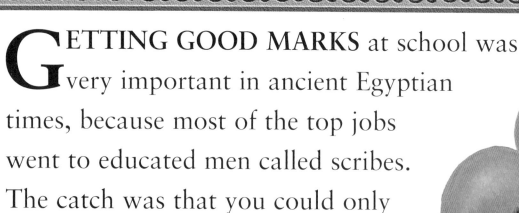

**GETTING GOOD MARKS** at school was very important in ancient Egyptian times, because most of the top jobs went to educated men called scribes. The catch was that you could only train as a scribe if you were a boy and your father was one already. Boys started school when they were five, and were ready to leave and begin work by the time they were twelve.

## CAN YOU BELIEVE IT?
*Boys were punished if they were naughty or lazy.*

**YES.** One ancient Egyptian saying warned that "a boy's ear is on his back" and that "he hears when he is beaten".

## WRITING ON REEDS

The ancient Egyptians wrote on an early kind of paper called papyrus, which was made from a river reed. Papyrus makers cut the reed stem into thin strips and layered the strips into a small sheet. The sheet was then beaten to join the layers, and dried in the sun.

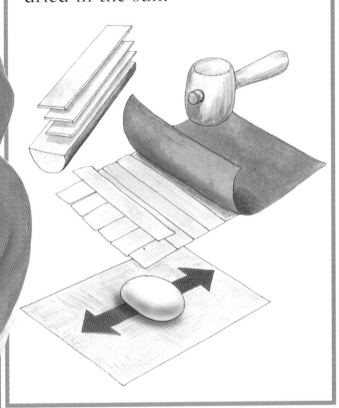

### *Picture perfect*

*Egyptians wrote with picture symbols called hieroglyphs instead of an alphabet made up of letters, and young scribes had to learn more than 700 of them off by heart.*

## YOU MUST BE JOKING!

Girls stayed at home, where they were taught weaving and other household skills by their mother. They married when they were about 14 – their husbands were aged 20 or so.

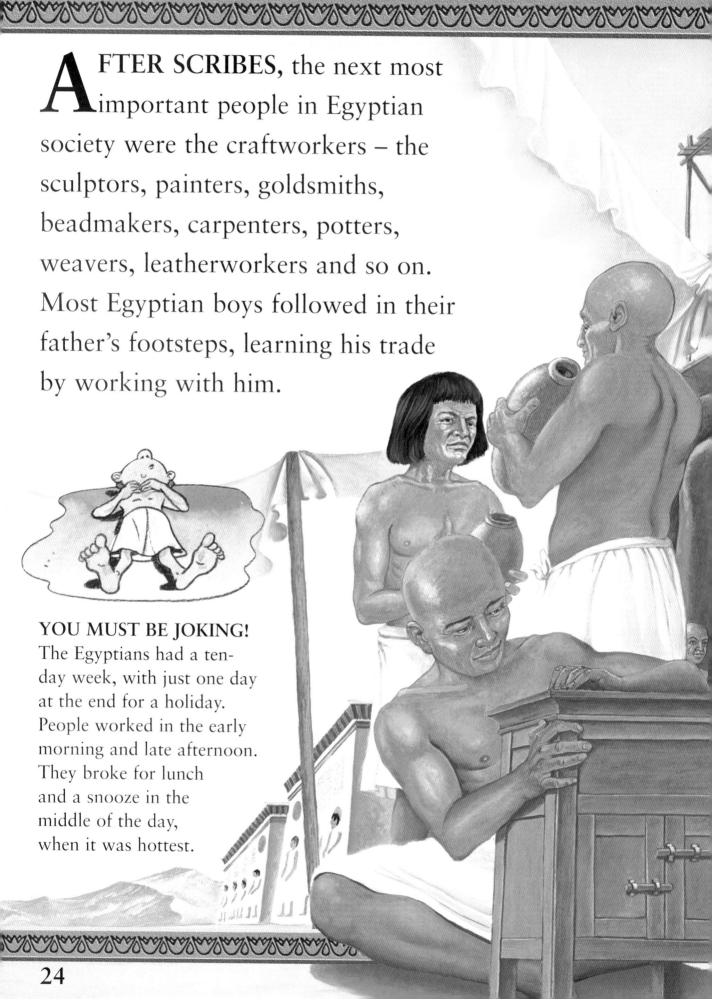

# CAREFUL CRAFTSMEN

**A**FTER SCRIBES, the next most important people in Egyptian society were the craftworkers – the sculptors, painters, goldsmiths, beadmakers, carpenters, potters, weavers, leatherworkers and so on. Most Egyptian boys followed in their father's footsteps, learning his trade by working with him.

**YOU MUST BE JOKING!**
The Egyptians had a ten-day week, with just one day at the end for a holiday. People worked in the early morning and late afternoon. They broke for lunch and a snooze in the middle of the day, when it was hottest.

**CAN YOU BELIEVE IT?**
*The Egyptians paid for goods with coins.*

**NO**. They didn't use money. Goods were bartered, or swapped.

FOR SALE

***Chip off the old block***
*Sculptors created statues in all sizes, from stone giants that took many years to carve, to tiny metal figurines that were cast in a mould.*

TOOL CHEST  There were no power tools in ancient Egyptian times, but carpenters worked with a wide range of hand tools, including chisels, drills, and saws. Few trees grew in Egypt, so most of the wood for building and making furniture was imported from foreign countries.

25

# FUN AND GAMES

**F**ROM FARMERS TO PHARAOHS, the ancient Egyptians loved to spend their free time hunting. A farmer might hunt for wild birds along the riverbank, trapping them in nets or hitting them with a boomerang-shaped throwing stick. But wealthy Egyptians sometimes went after a bigger catch – a crocodile or a hippopotamus!

### YOU MUST BE JOKING!

The Egyptians' favourite board game was called *senet*, and it was rather like draughts. People who couldn't afford a special board, scratched the shape into the sand and used pebbles for pieces.

### CHILD'S PLAY

Some of the children's games from ancient Egyptian times are still played today – leapfrog, for instance, and tug-of-war. Children also had lots of home-made toys to play with, from balls and spinning tops to wooden animals with moving parts.

**CAN YOU BELIEVE IT?**
*Wealthy Egyptians hunted lions in the desert.*

**YES.** Hunters chased after the lions in chariots, and shot at them with bows and arrows.

*Sporting chance*
*Hunters diced with death, trying to spear fierce river creatures from a small reed boat. An angry hippo could easily tip the boat over. And if you fell in, there were the crocodiles to worry about!*

# WATERY HIGHWAY

**B**OATS WERE HUGELY IMPORTANT in ancient Egyptian times, and not just for hunting. The Nile River was the country's main highway, and most people travelled by water. Different boats were used for fishing and hunting, travelling, and transporting goods and animals. The smallest and simplest boats were made from bundles of river reeds, but larger ones were built from wood.

## YOU MUST BE JOKING!
Winds usually blow from the north to the south of Egypt. So people sailed their boats when travelling southward and rowed them northward. Like people's clothes, sails were made of linen.

## River traffic

*The Nile was almost as busy as a modern-day motorway. Most towns had a riverside quay, while temples and palaces had their own private harbour, linked to the river by a canal.*

## SHIP OF DEATH

The Egyptians believed that the dead needed boats in the Afterlife, and the pieces for a 43-metre-long ship were buried in a pit beside Pharaoh Khufu's Great Pyramid at Giza. Each of the 1,244 pieces was labelled so that the ship could be put back together by the pharaoh's servants when he reached the Afterlife.

**CAN YOU BELIEVE IT?**
*Egyptian gods travelled in boats.*

**YES.** The Egyptians believed that Ra, their sun god, sailed across the sky each day.

# GOING TO WAR

**A**LTHOUGH THE EGYPTIANS were a peaceable lot, from time to time they had to go to war against a neighbouring country. The army was made up of foot and chariot troops. Each chariot was manned by a driver and a bowman, who fired arrows at the enemy. Foot soldiers fought with spears, daggers and battle axes, and carried a shield to protect themselves.

*Battle order*
*When a battle began, the foot soldiers usually led the charge, with the charioteers following on behind.*

**CAN YOU BELIEVE IT?**

*The bravest soldiers won medals.*

**YES.** The medal was fly-shaped and made of gold.

## YOU MUST BE JOKING!

After winning a battle, the Egyptians would cut off bits of their dead enemies' bodies, such as a hand or a tongue. This allowed scribes to count how many enemies had been killed.

## WARRIOR KINGS

Although the pharaoh was head of the army, only some were brave enough to lead their troops into war. Even so, many pharaohs commissioned wall-paintings or carvings to portray themselves as warriors. Some were outrageous bigheads – Ramesses III, for example, boasted that he'd killed more than 12,500 enemies in a single battle!

# INDEX